2015 GREATEST POP & MOVIE HITS

ARRANGED BY
DAN COATES

CONTENTS

Produced by
Alfred Music
P.O. Box 10003
Van Nuys, CA 91410-0003
alfred.com

Printed in USA.

ISBN-10: 1-4706-2325-0
ISBN-13: 978-1-4706-2325-8

Cover Photo: © Shutterstock.com / Vladitto

19 YOU + ME

Words and Music by Dan Smyers,
Shay Mooney and Danny Orton
Arr. Dan Coates

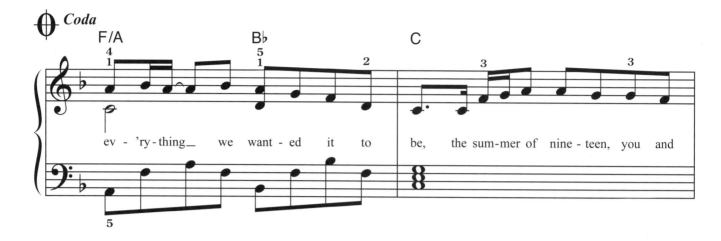

ev - 'ry-thing__ we want - ed it to be, the sum-mer of nine - teen, you and

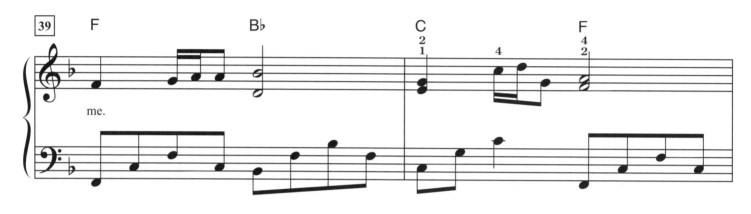

me.

First week, Myr - tle Beach,__ where it all__ be - gan.

Verse 2:
We had our first dance in the sand,
It was one hell of a souvenir.
Tangled up, so in love, and so let's just stay right here.
Till the sun starts creepin', creepin' up,
Right then I knew just what you were thinkin', thinkin' of
When I looked at you.
(To Chorus:)

AIN'T IT FUN

Words and Music by
Hayley Williams and Taylor York
Arr. Dan Coates

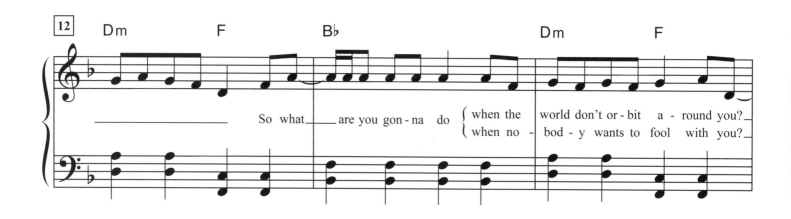

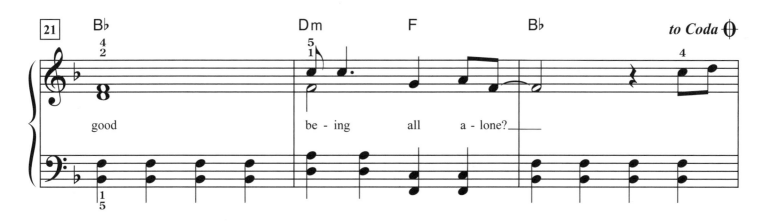

good

be - ing all a - lone?

1.

2.

2. Where you're

Ain't it good to be on your own? Ain't it

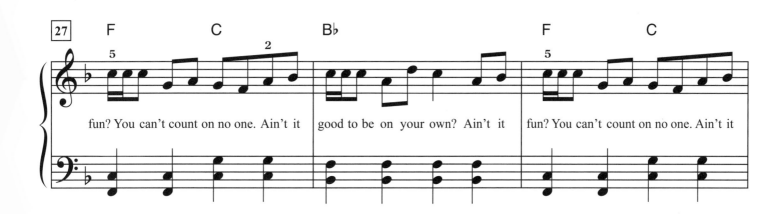

fun? You can't count on no one. Ain't it good to be on your own? Ain't it fun? You can't count on no one. Ain't it

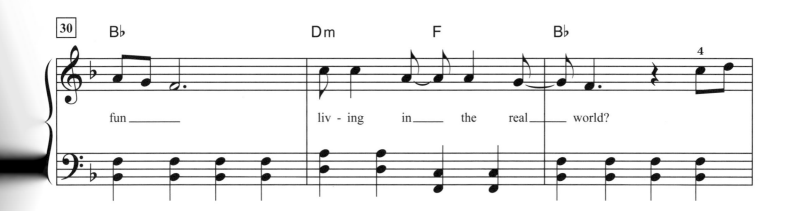

fun living in the real world?

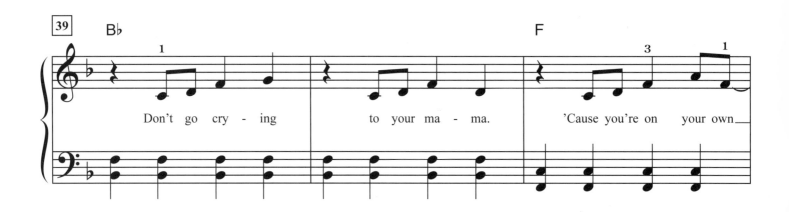

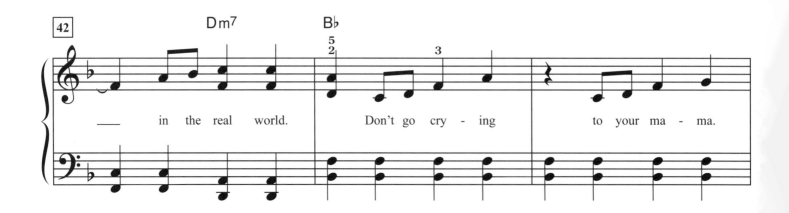

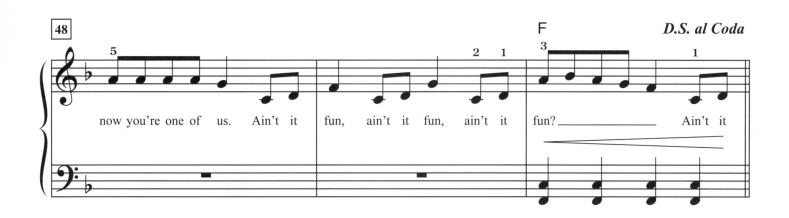

ALL ABOUT THAT BASS

Words and Music by
Meghan Trainor and Kevin Kadish

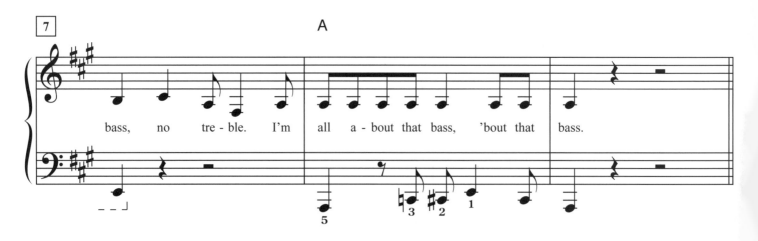

Verses:

1. Yeah, it's pret-ty clear,
2. *See additional lyrics.*

I ain't no size two, but I can shake it, shake it

like I'm sup-posed to do. 'Cause I got that boom, boom that all the boys chase. And all

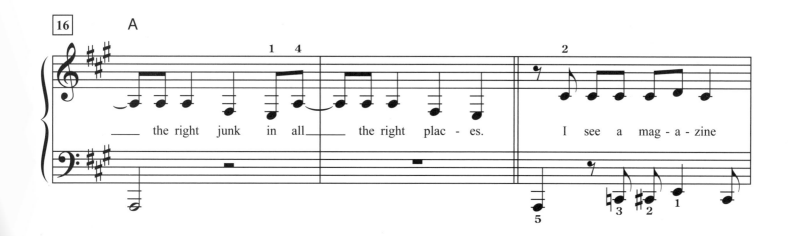

___ the right junk in all___ the right plac - es. I see a mag - a - zine

work-ing that Pho - to - shop.___ We know that **** ain't real, come on now, make it stop.

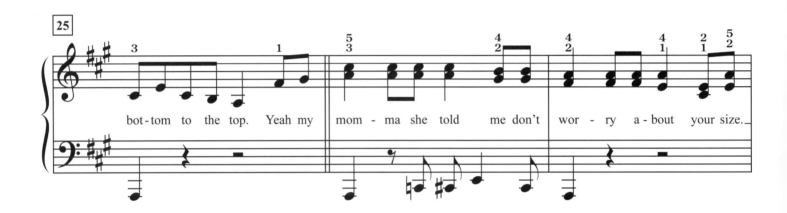

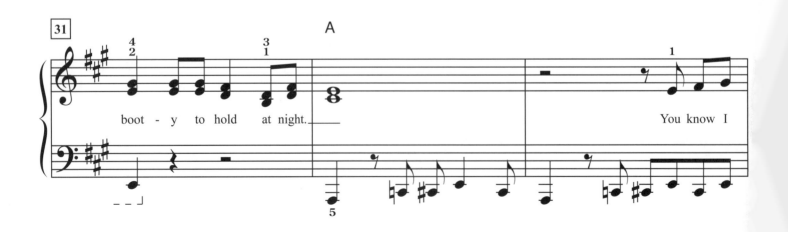

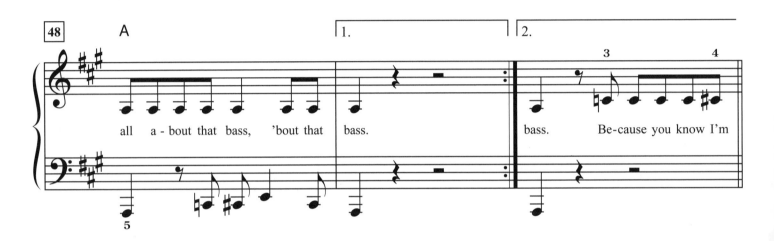

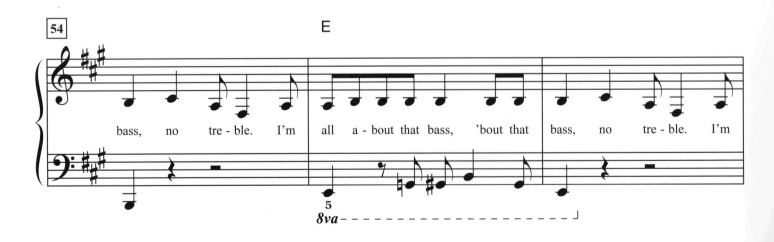

all a-bout that bass, 'bout that bass. Be-cause you know I'm bass.

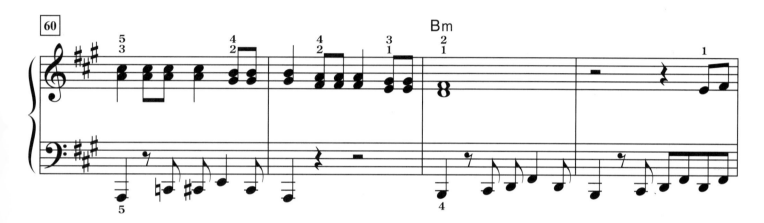

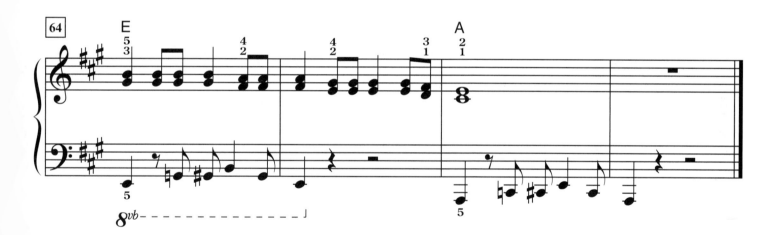

Verse 2:
I'm bringing booty back.
Go ahead and tell them skinny ******* that.
No, I'm just playing. I know you think you're fat,
But I'm here to tell you, ev'ry inch of you is perfect
From the bottom to the top.

ALONE YET NOT ALONE

Music by Bruce Broughton
Lyrics by Dennis Spiegel
Arr. Dan Coates

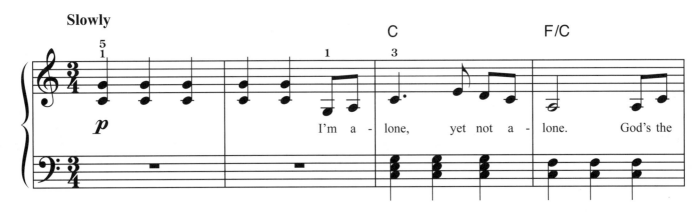

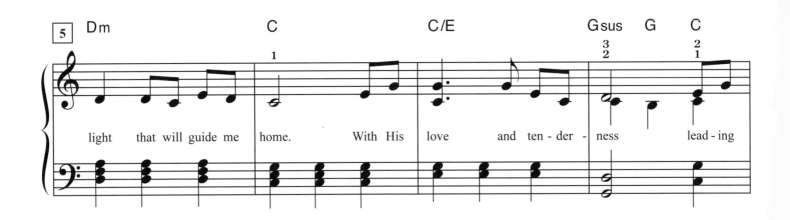

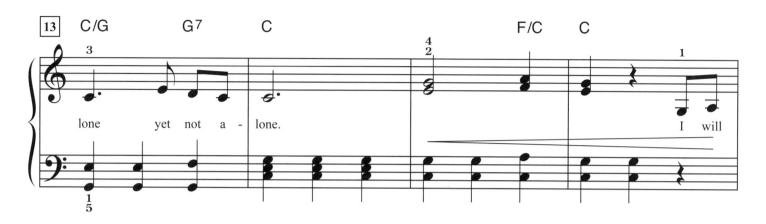

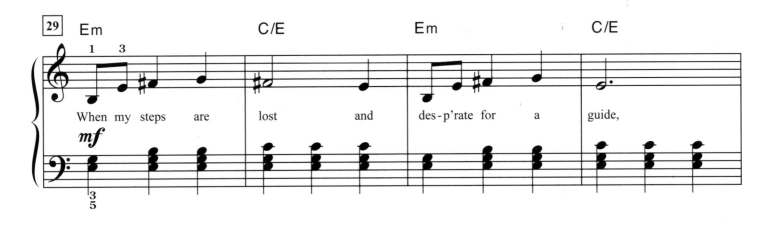

When my steps are lost and des-p'rate for a guide,

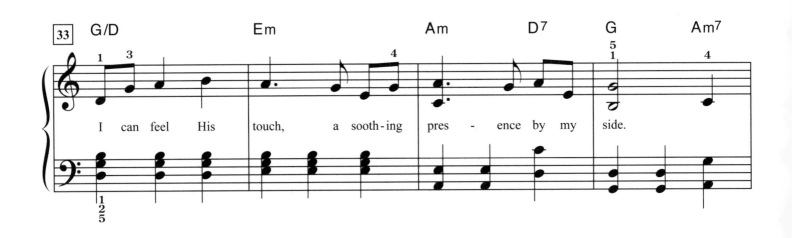

I can feel His touch, a sooth-ing pres - ence by my side.

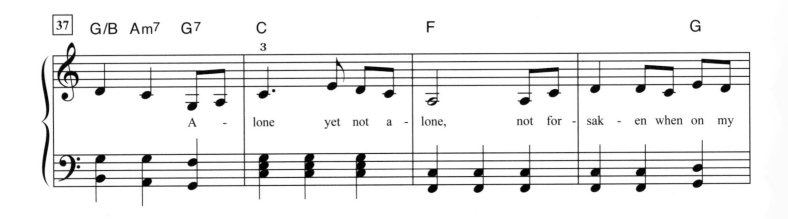

A - lone yet not a - lone, not for - sak - en when on my

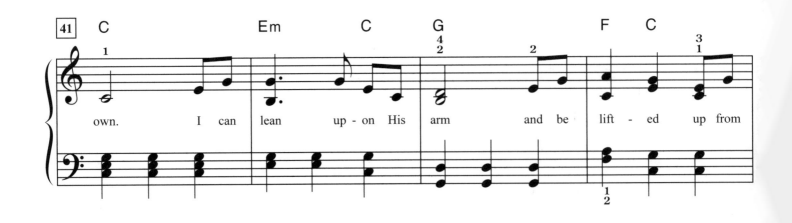

own. I can lean up - on His arm and be lift - ed up from

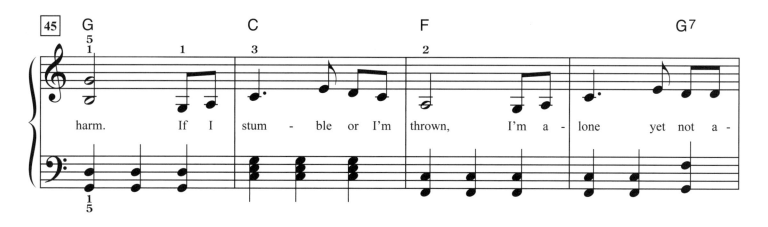

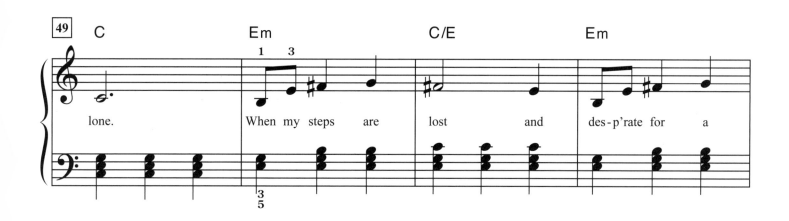

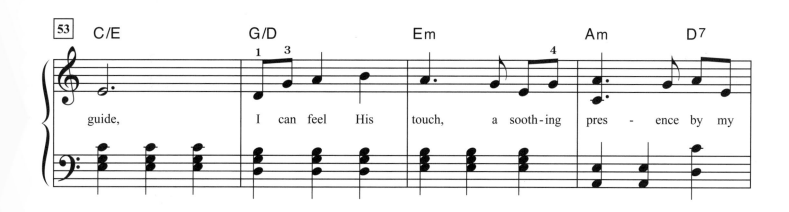

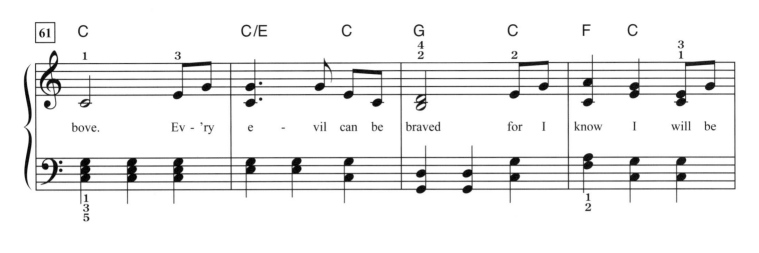

bove. Ev - 'ry e - vil can be braved for I know I will be

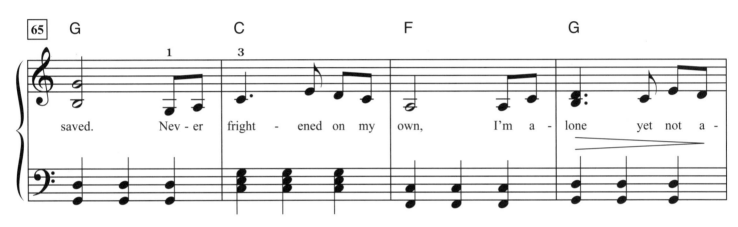

saved. Nev - er fright - ened on my own, I'm a - lone yet not a -

lone. I'm a - lone yet

not a - lone.

BEST DAY OF MY LIFE

Words and Music by Zachary Barnett,
James Adam Shelley, Matthew Sanchez,
David Rublin, Shep Goodman and Aaron Accetta
Arr. Dan Coates

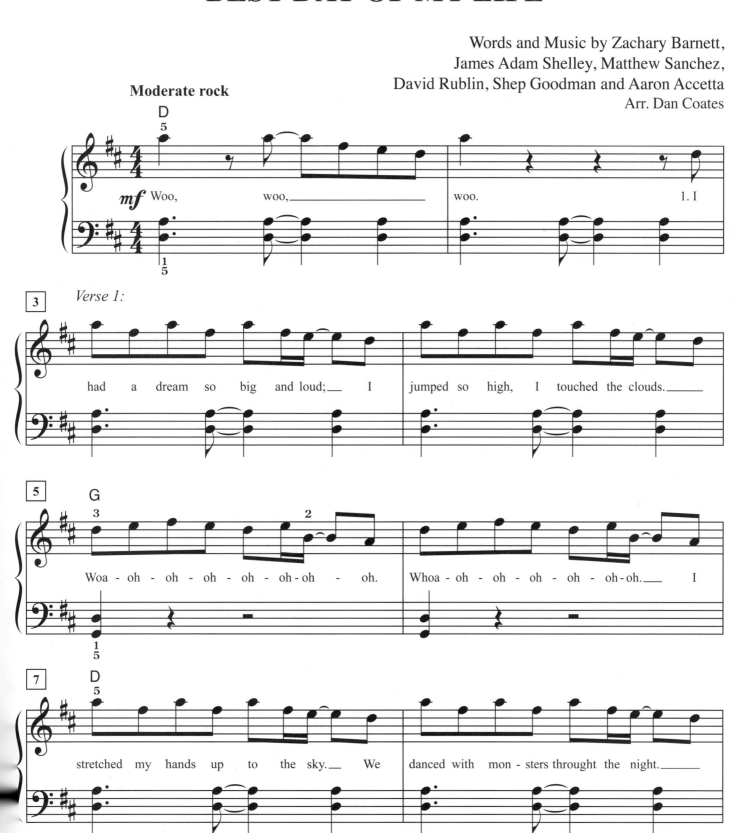

26

BELIEVER

Words and Music by Zachary Barnett,
James Adam Shelley, Matthew Sanchez,
David Rublin, Shep Goodman and Aaron Accetta
Arr. Dan Coates

Moderate rock

Chorus:

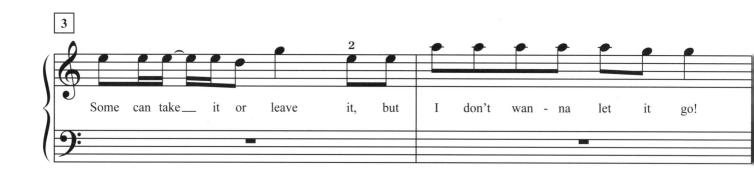

Verse 1:

BEYOND THE FOREST

(from *The Hobbit: The Desolation of Smaug*)

Music by Howard Shore
Lyrics by Philippa Boyens
Arr. Dan Coates

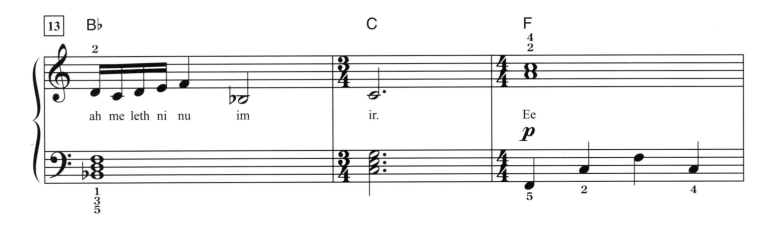

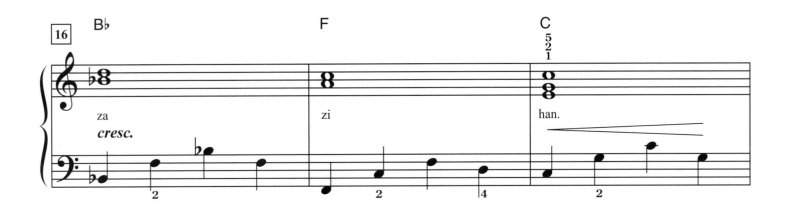

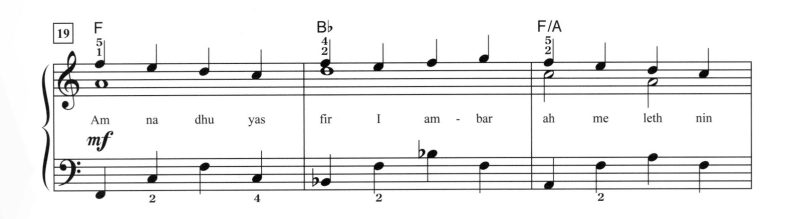

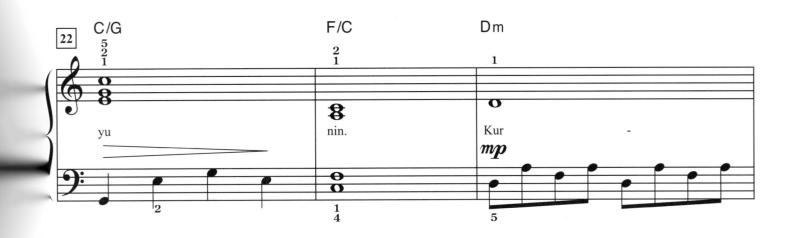

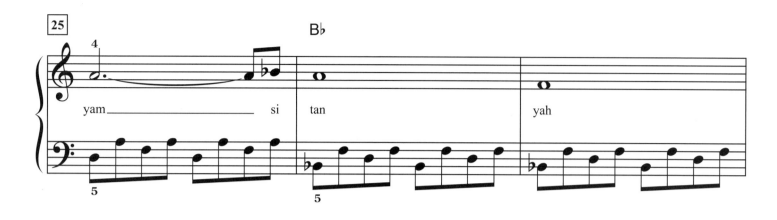

yam_____ si tan yah

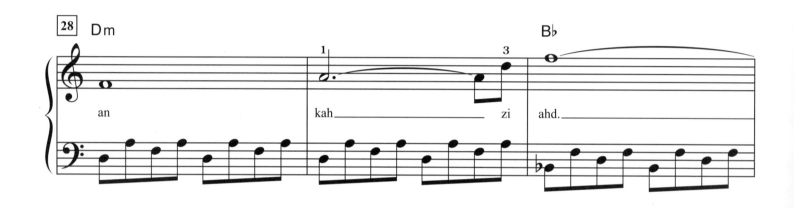

an kah_____ zi ahd.

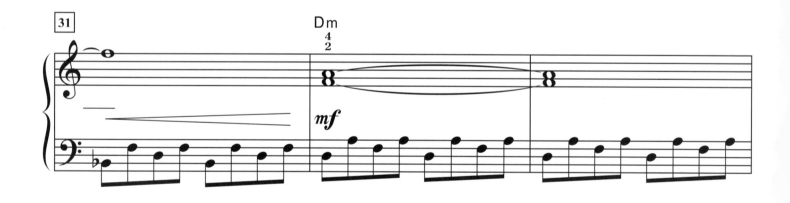

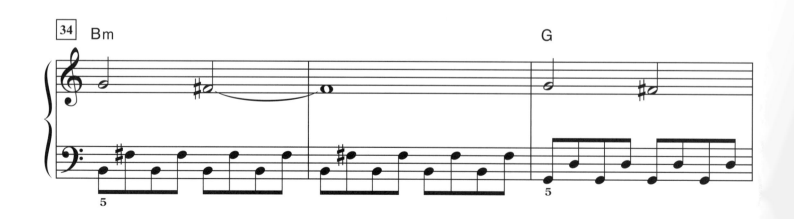

BLEED FOR LOVE

(from *Winnie Mandela*)

Words and Music by Diane Warren
Arr. Dan Coates

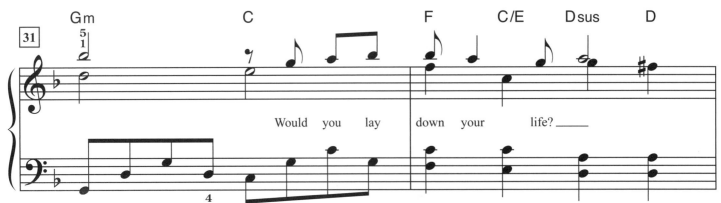

CAN YOU HEAR YOUR HEART?

(from *Winter's Tale*)

Music by Hans Zimmer,
Ann Marie Calhoun and Rupert Gregson-Williams
Arr. Dan Coates

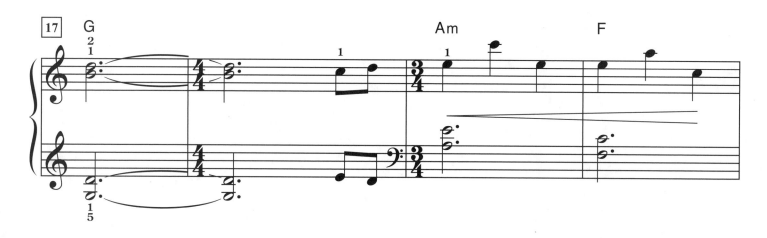

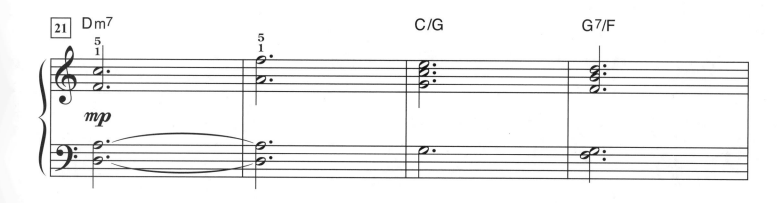

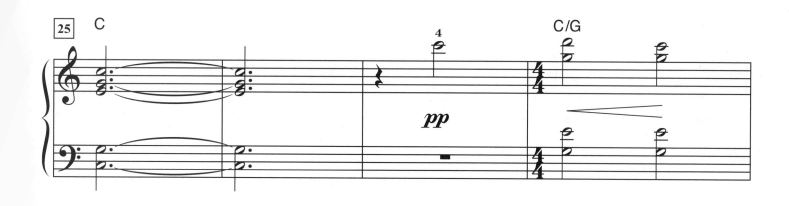

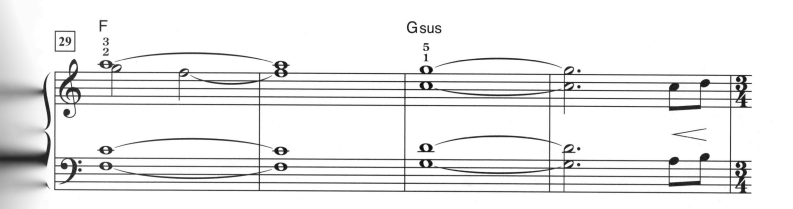

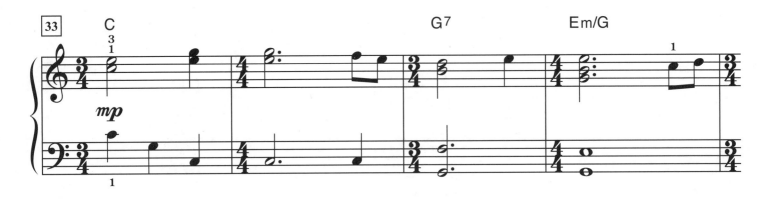

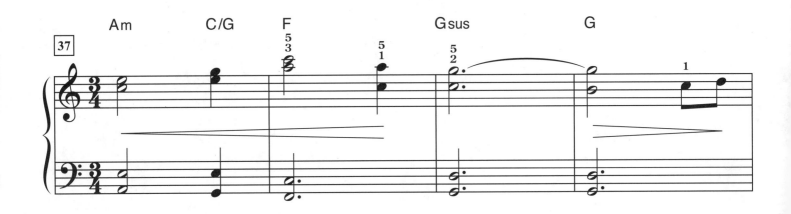

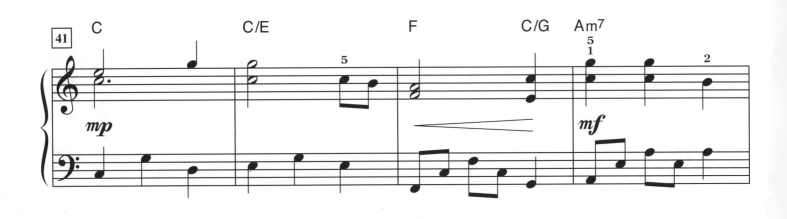

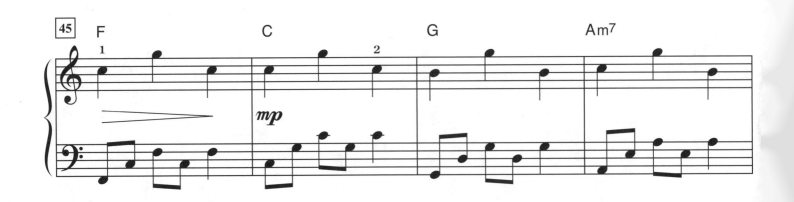

CLOUDS

Words and Music by Zach Sobiech
Arr. Dan Coates

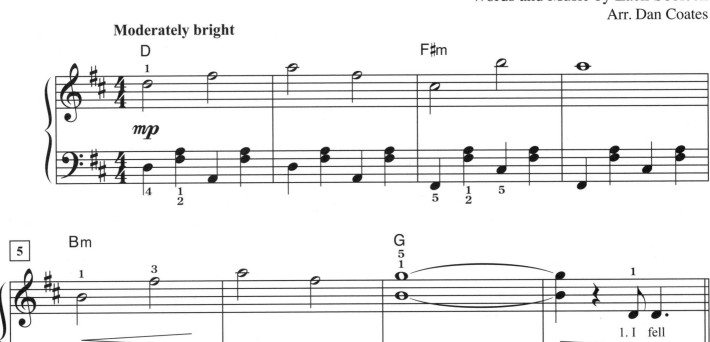

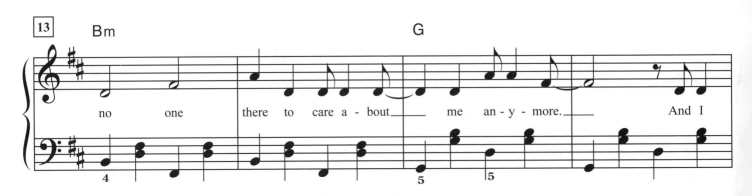

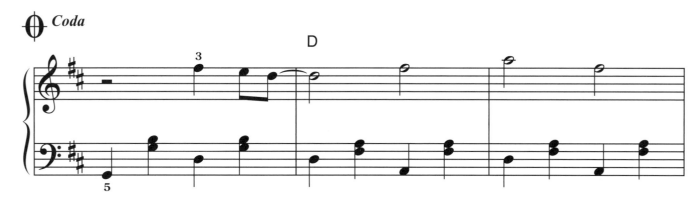

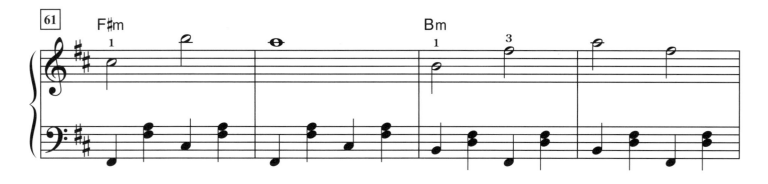

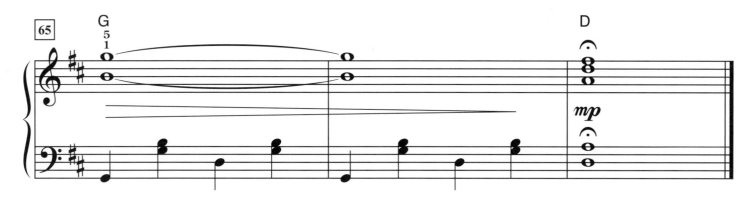

Verse 2:
When we get back on land,
Well, I'll never get my chance,
Be ready to live and it'll be
Ripped right out of my hands.
And maybe some day
We'll take a little ride,
We'll go up, up, up
And everything will be just fine.
(To Chorus:)

Verse 3:
We could go up, up, up,
Up and take that little ride,
We'll sit there holding hands
And everything would be just right.
And maybe someday
I'll see you again,
We'll float up in the clouds
And we'll never see the end.
(To Chorus:)

COMING UP ROSES

(from *Begin Again*)

Words and Music by
Glen Hansard and Danielle Brisebois
Arr. Dan Coates

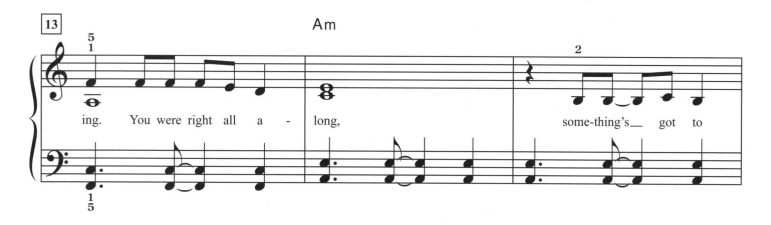

ing. You were right all a - long, some-thing's__ got to

Chorus:

change. Hold

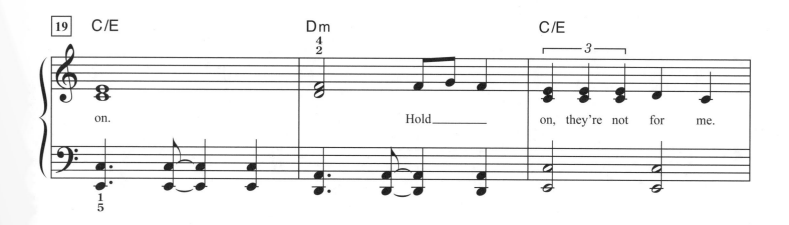

on. Hold_____ on, they're not for me.

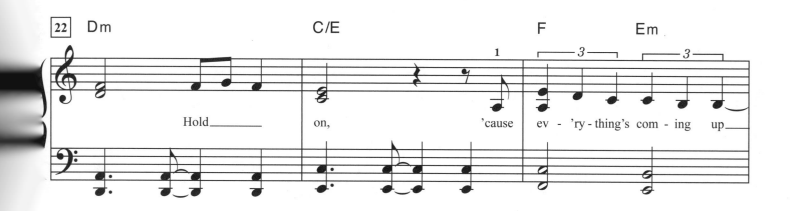

Hold_____ on, 'cause ev - 'ry-thing's com - ing up__

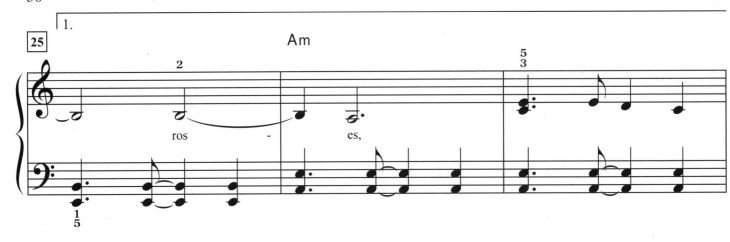

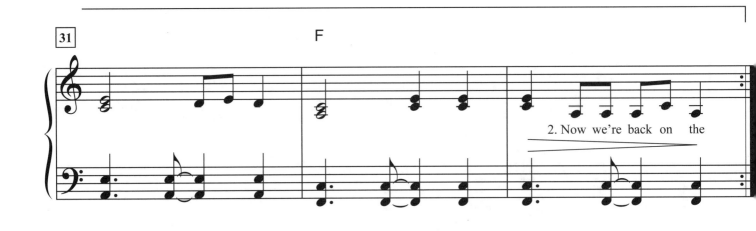

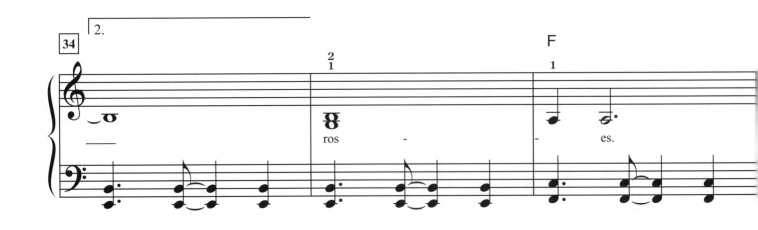

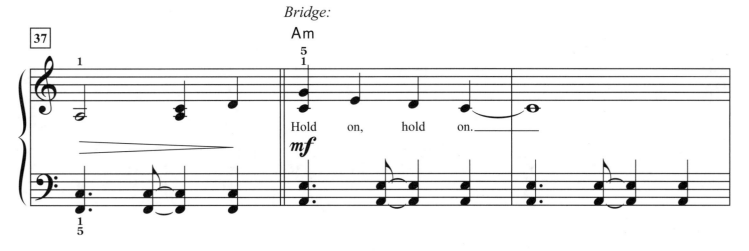

Bridge:

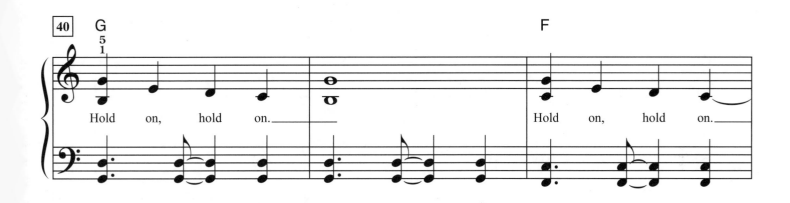

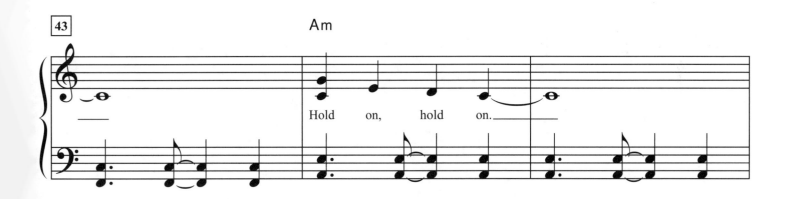

Verse 2:
Now we're back on the street,
Found a song that's worth singing.
The blur that knows a defeat
While your victory bell's ringing.
My whole life's turned around,
For this thing you keep chasing.
You were right all along,
But it's me who's got to change.
(To Chorus:)

COMPASS

Words and Music by Diane Warren
Arr. Dan Coates

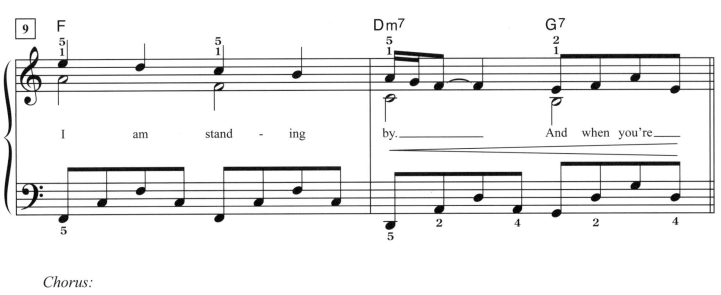

I am stand - ing by. _____ And when you're _____

Chorus:

lost and think no one can find you, I will re -

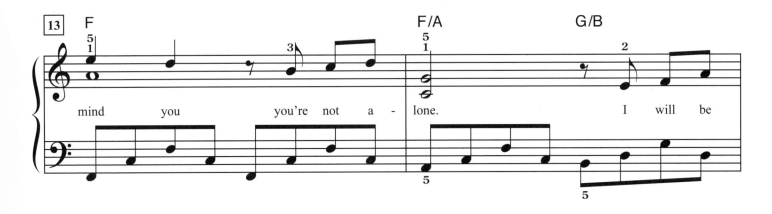

mind you you're not a - lone. I will be

there, I'll be the one to guide you. My love will be your

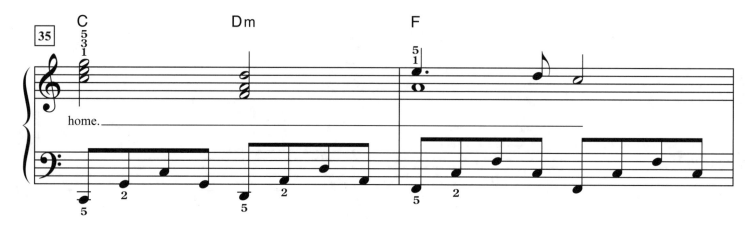

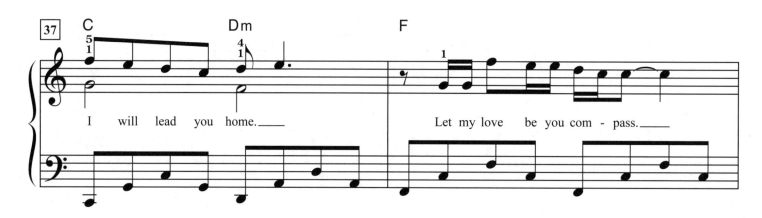

Verse 2:
When night has painted
Your world in shadows,
And you're left feeling left out in the cold,
When you're in the darkness
And this world feels heartless,
I will see you, hear you, reach you.
I am standing by.
(To Chorus:)

DOIN' WHAT SHE LIKES

Words and Music by
Wade Kirby and Phil O'Donnell
Arr. Dan Coates

Moderately slow

Verse:

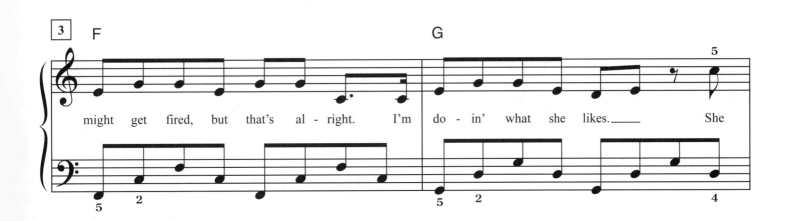

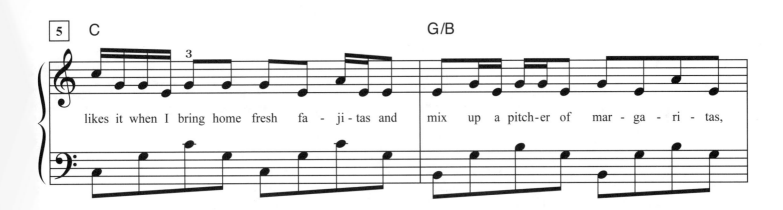

15 F · · · · · G · · · · · *to Coda* ⊕

let-tin' them burn and hold - in' her___ all night._____ I like do - in' what she

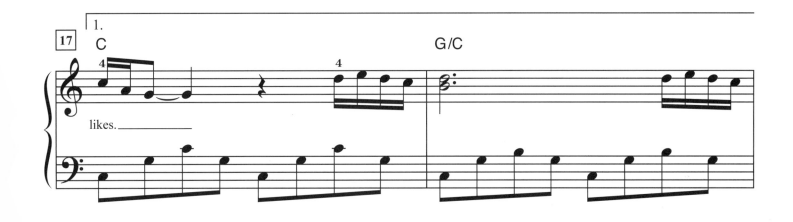

1.
17 C · · · · · G/C

likes._____

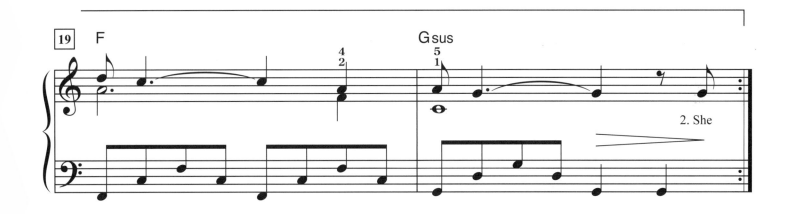

19 F · · · · · Gsus

2. She

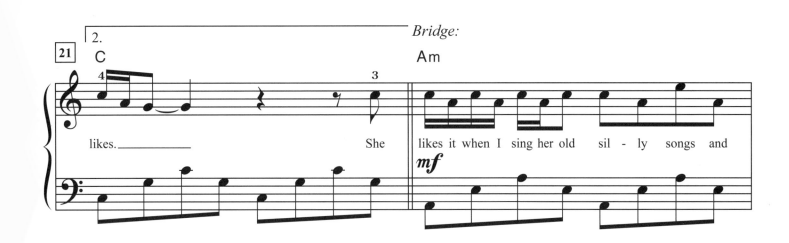

2. *Bridge:*
21 C · · · · · Am

likes._____ She likes it when I sing her old sil - ly songs and

mf

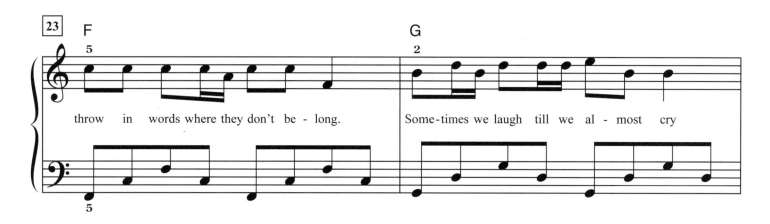

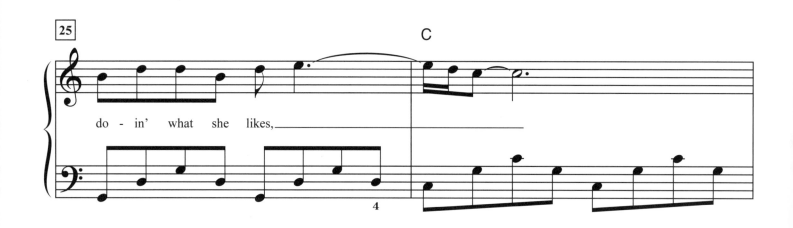

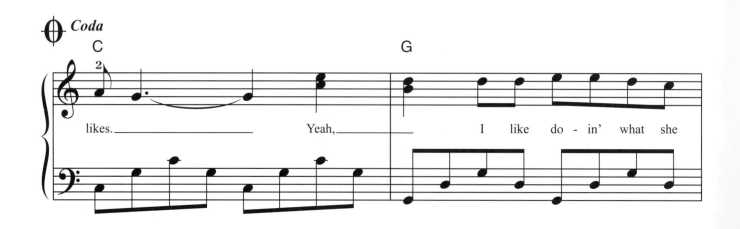

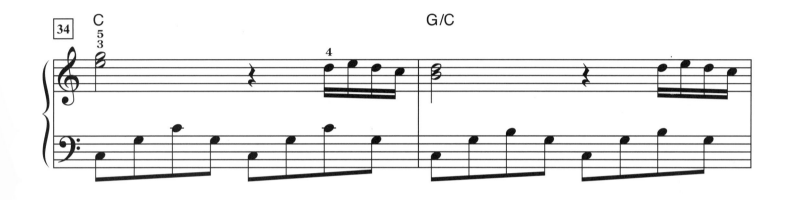

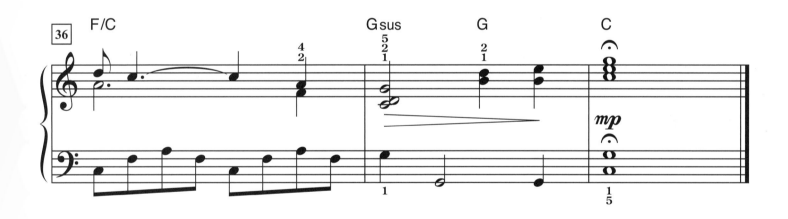

Verse 2:
She likes it when I get past second gear,
Sees gravel flying in the rearview mirror.
Sometimes I'm pushin' ninety five
Doin' what she likes.
And she likes it when I find a road that's dark.
Can we pull off somewhere and park?
Turn the radio on and turn off the lights;
Keep doin' what she likes.
(To Chorus:)

COOL KIDS

Words and Music by Graham Sierota,
Jamie Sierota, Noah Sierota, Sydney Sierota,
Jeffery David Sierota and Jesiah Dzwonek
Arr. Dan Coates

Moderate rock

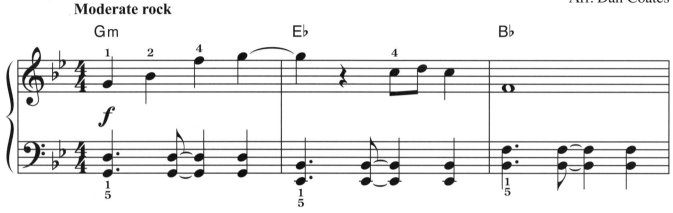

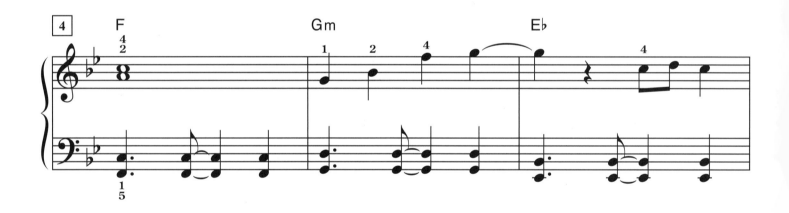

Verse:

1. She sees them walk-ing in a straight line;
2. *See additional lyrics.*

that's not real-ly her style. And they all

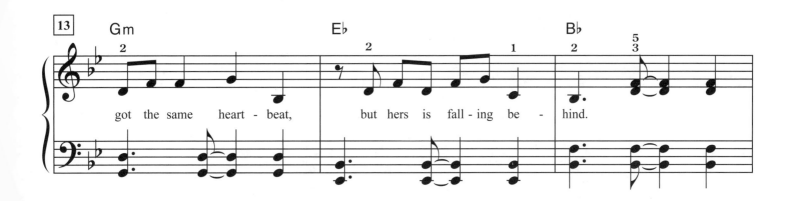

got the same heart-beat, but hers is fall-ing be - hind.

Noth-ing in this world could ev - er bring____ them

down. Yeah, they're in - vin - ci - ble,

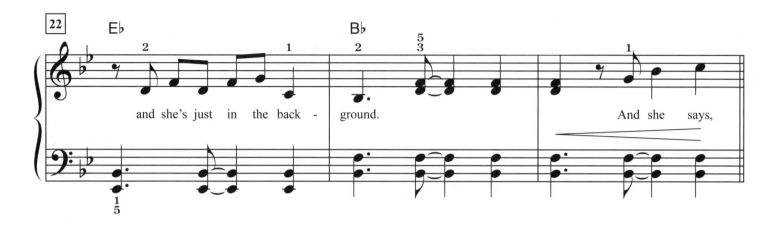

and she's just in the back - ground. And she says,

Chorus:

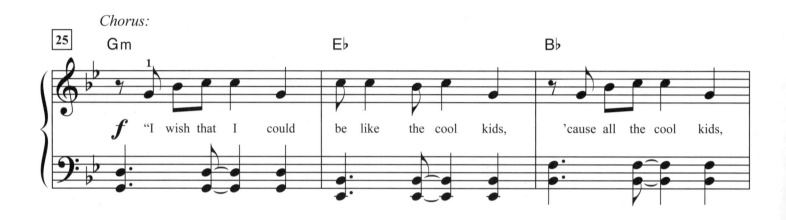

f "I wish that I could be like the cool kids, 'cause all the cool kids,

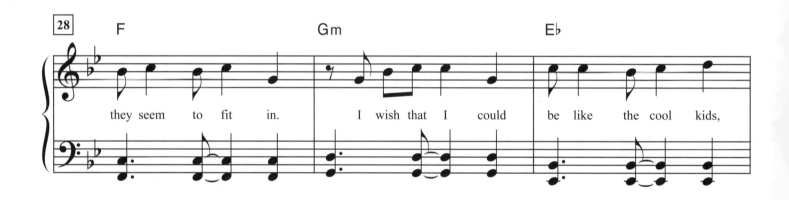

they seem to fit in. I wish that I could be like the cool kids,

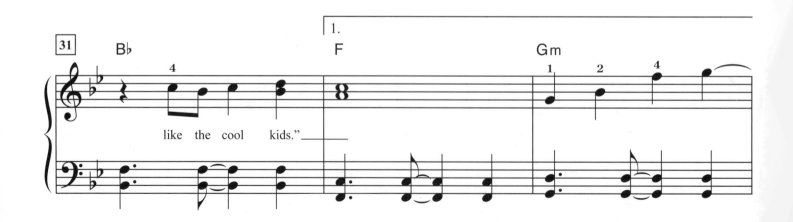

like the cool kids."

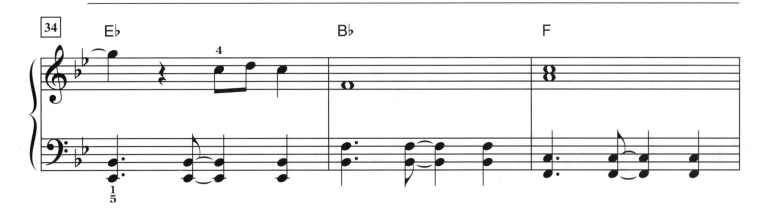

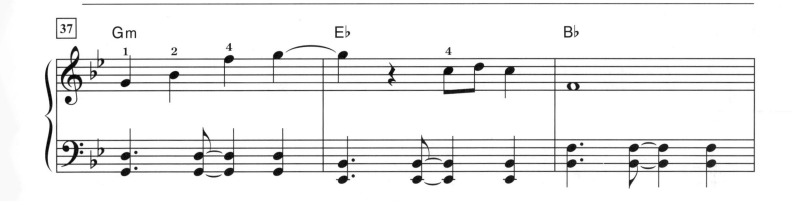

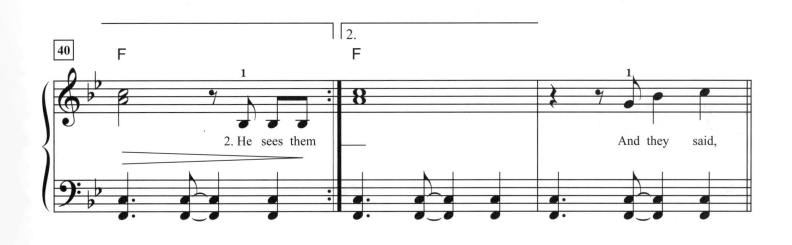

2. He sees them

And they said,

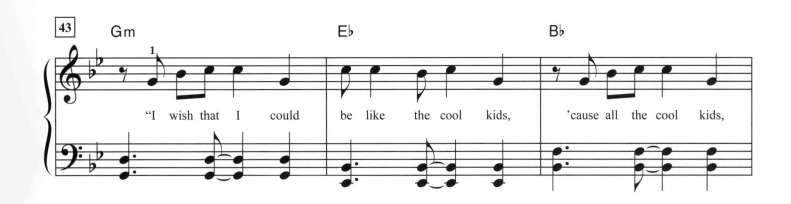

"I wish that I could be like the cool kids, 'cause all the cool kids,

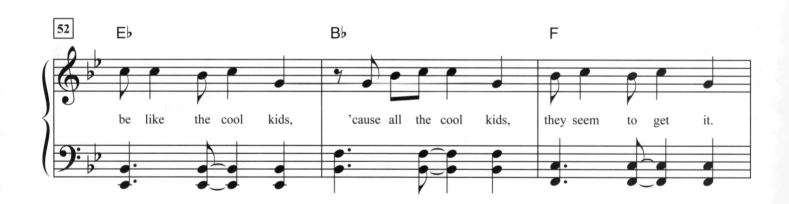

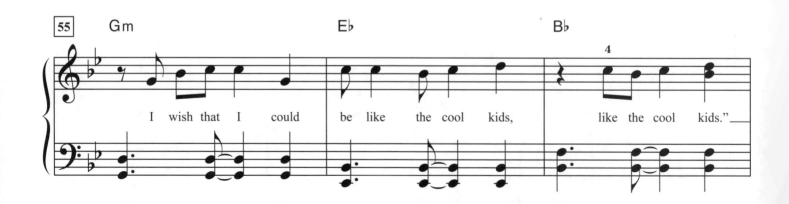

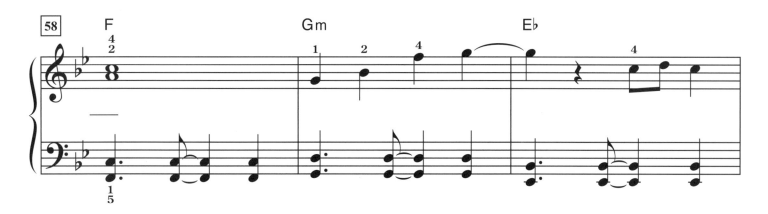

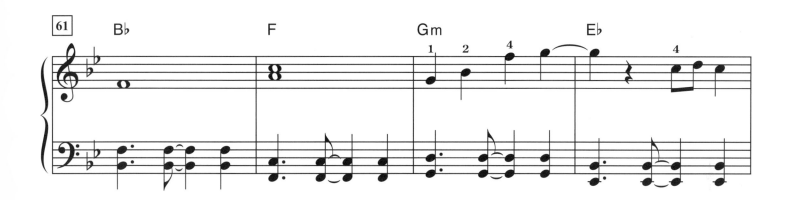

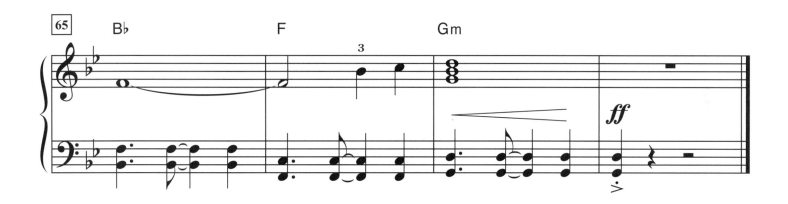

Verse 2:
He sees them talking with a big smile,
but they haven't got a clue.
Yeah, they're living the good life;
Can't see what he is going through.
They're driving fast cars,
But they don't know where they're going;
In the fast lane, living life without knowing.
And he says,
(To Chorus:)

EVERYTHING I DIDN'T SAY

Words and Music by Ashton Irwin, John Feldmann,
Calum Hood and Nicholas Ras Furlong
Arr. Dan Coates

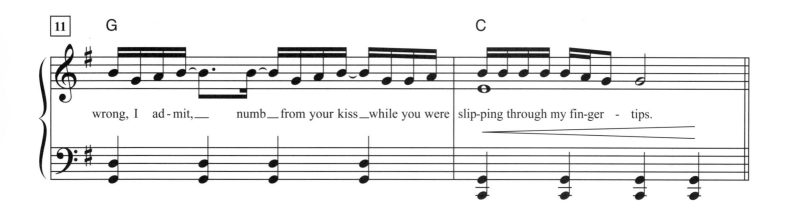

Chorus:

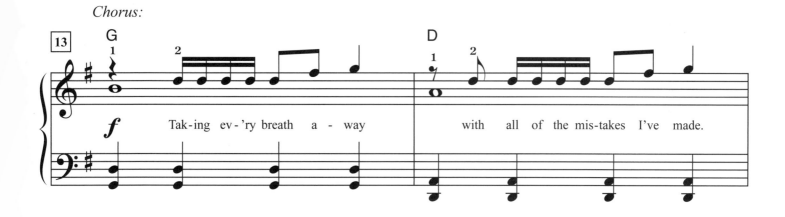

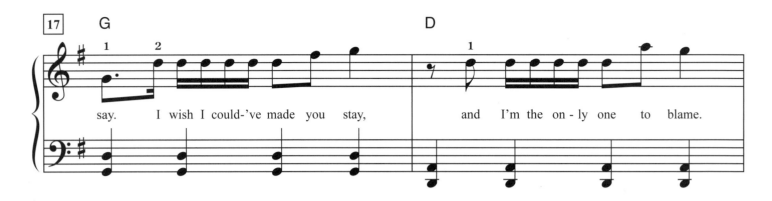

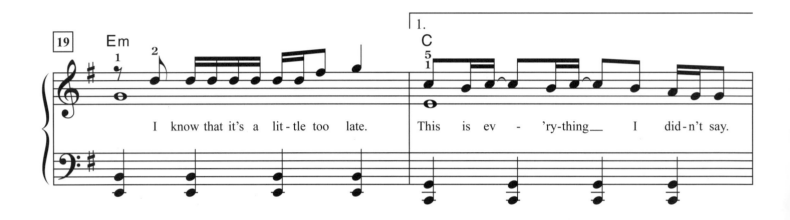

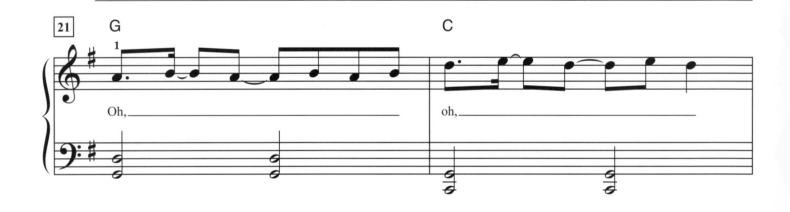

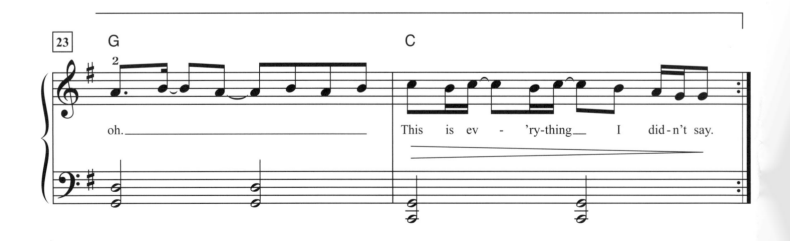

Bridge:

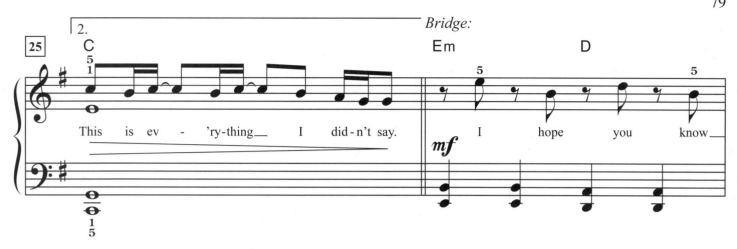

25 | C | Em | D

This is ev - 'ry-thing___ I did-n't say. I hope you know___

27 | C | Em | D

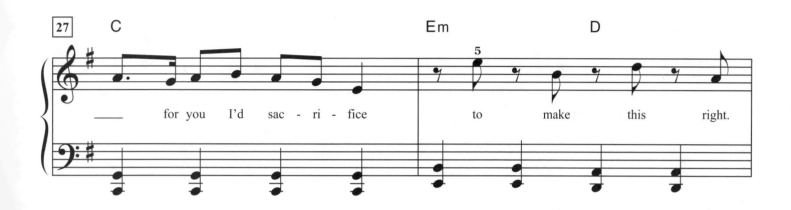

___ for you I'd sac - ri - fice to make this right.

29 | C | Em | D

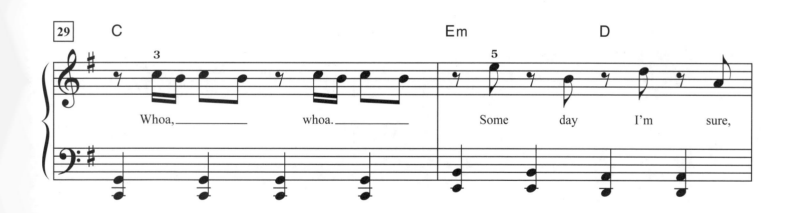

Whoa,_____ whoa._____ Some day I'm sure,

31 | C | Em | D

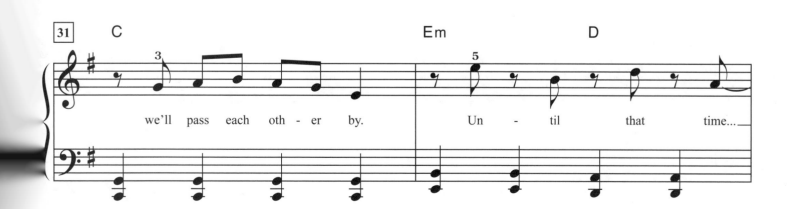

we'll pass each oth - er by. Un - til that time...___

Chorus:

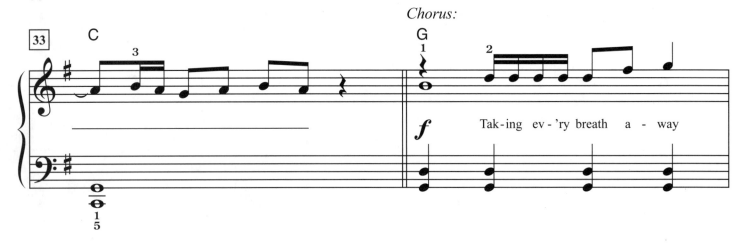

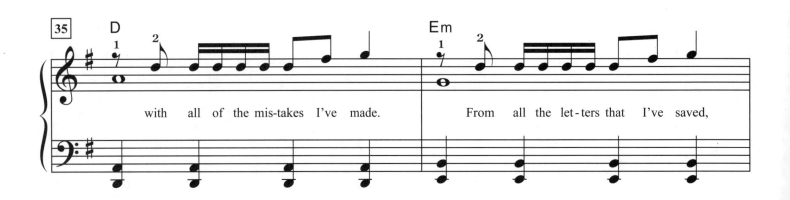

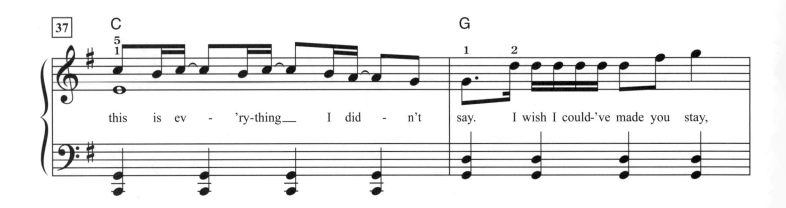

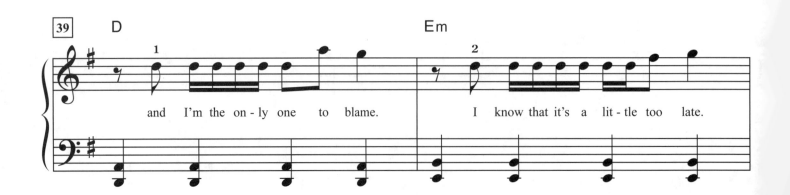

Verse 2:
Wake me up, now and tell me this is all a bad dream.
All the songs that I wrote, all the wrongs that I hoped
Would erase from your memory.
Holding on to a broken and empty heart.
Flowers I should have bought, all the hours I lost,
Wish I could bring it back to the start.
(To Chorus:)

EVERYTHING IS AWESOME
(AWESOME REMIXXX!!!)

(from *The Lego Movie*)

Music by Shawn Patterson
Lyrics by Shawn Patterson, Andy Samberg,
Akiva Schaffer, Jorma Taccone,
Joshua Bartholomew and Lisa Harriton
Arr. Dan Coates

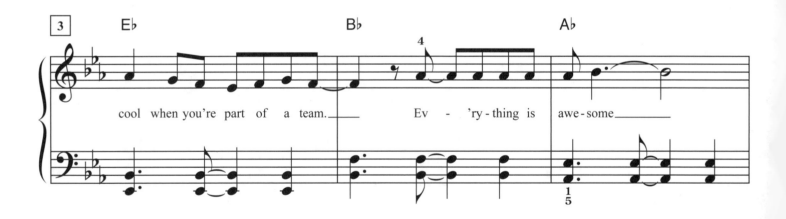

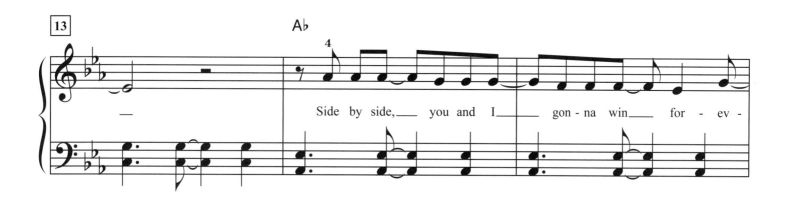

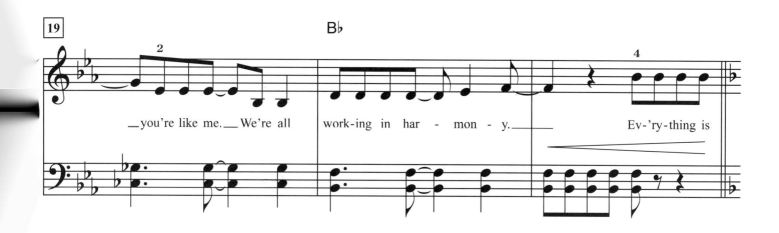

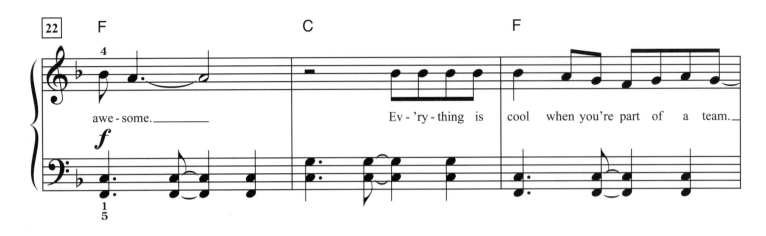

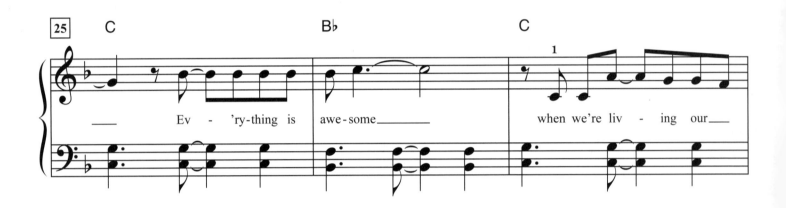

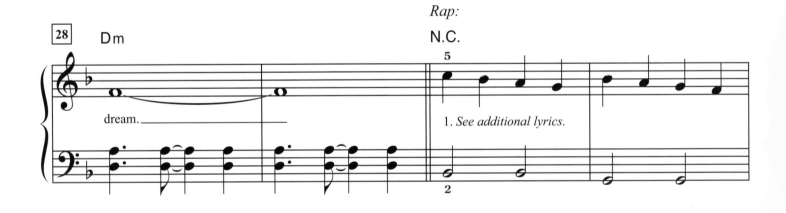

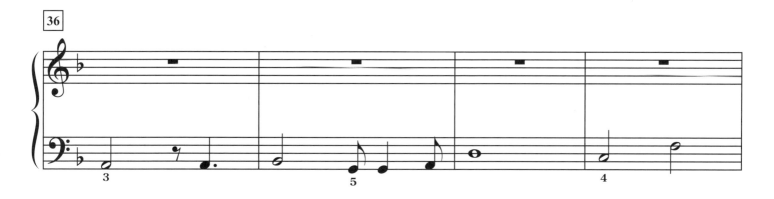

Bridge:

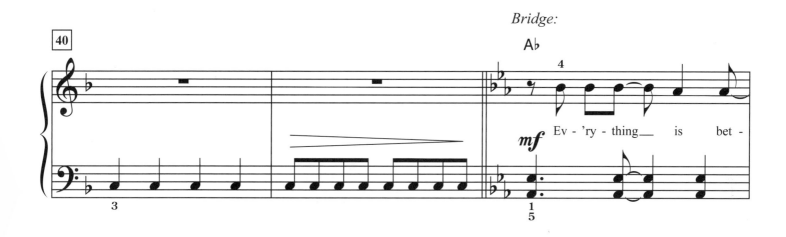

Ev - 'ry - thing__ is bet -

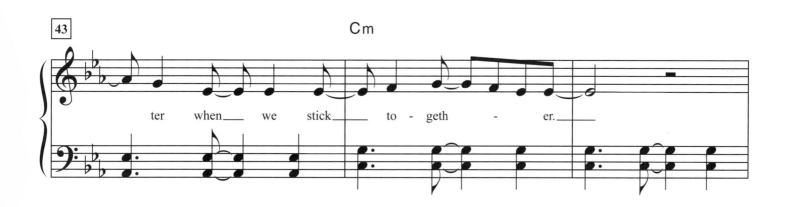

ter when__ we stick__ to - geth - er.__

Side by side,__ you and I__ gon - na win__ for - ev - er. Let's par - ty for - ev -

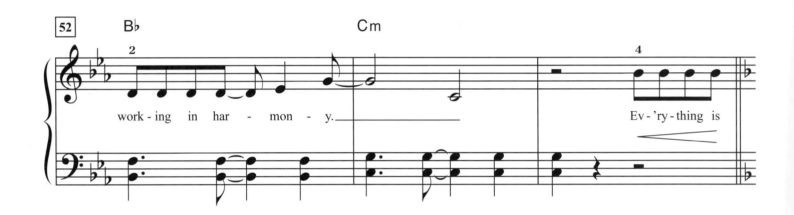

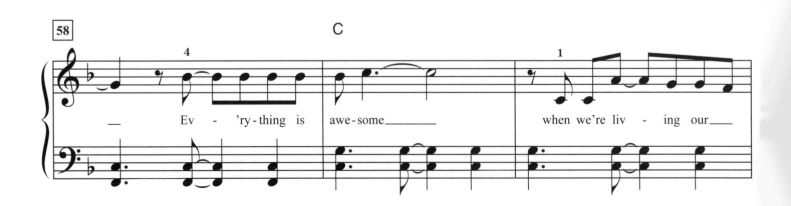

Rap:

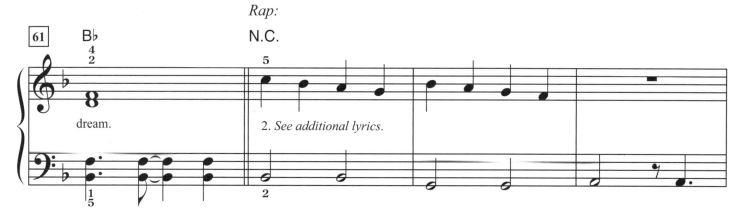

dream.

2. *See additional lyrics.*

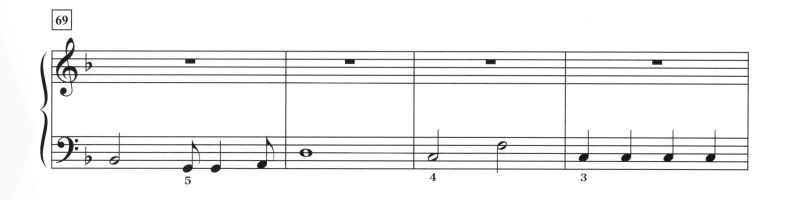

Chorus:

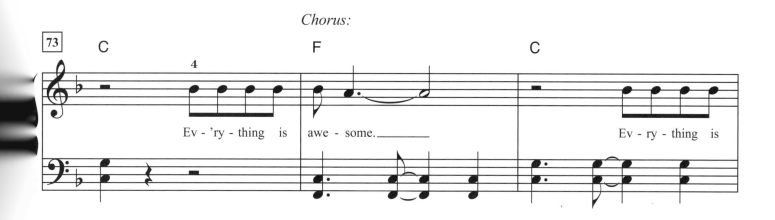

Ev - 'ry - thing is   awe - some._____   Ev - ry - thing is

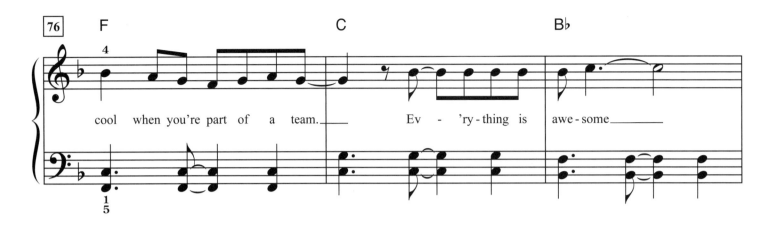

Rap 1:

Have you heard the news? Everyone's talkin'.
Life is good cause everything's awesome.
Lost my job, there's a new opportunity,
More free time for my awesome community.
I feel more awesome than an awesome possum,
Dip my body in chocolate frostin'.
Three years later, washed out the frostin',
Smellin' like a blossom, everything is awesome.
Stepped in mud, got new brown shoes.
It's awesome to win and it's awesome to lose.
(To Bridge:)

Rap 2:

Blue skies, bouncy springs,
We just named two awesome things.
A Nobel Prize, a piece of string.
You know what's awesome? EVERYTHING!
Dogs with fleas,
Allergies,
A book of Greek antiquities,
Brand new pants, a very old vest,
Awesome items are the best.
Trees, frogs, clogs, they're awesome!
Rocks, clocks, and socks, they're awesome!
Figs and jigs and twigs, that's awesome!
Everything you see or think or say is awesome!
(To Chorus:)

GRAVITY

Composed by Steven Price
Arr. Dan Coates

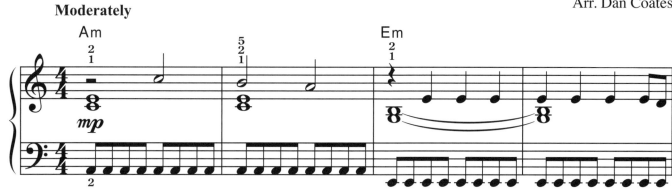

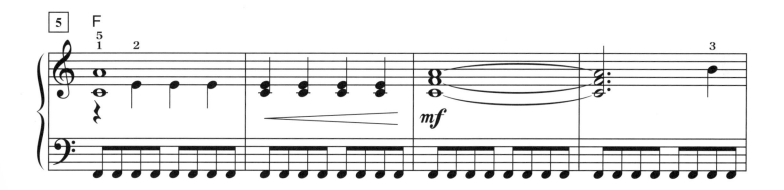

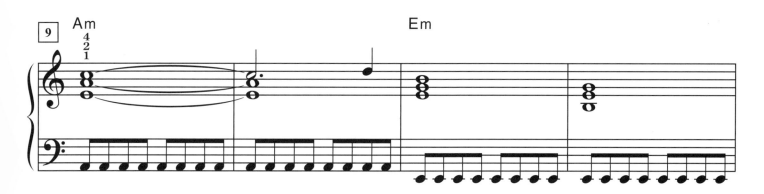

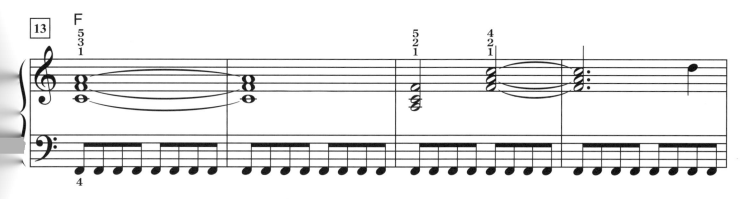

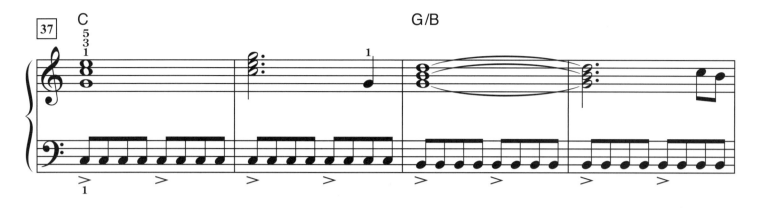

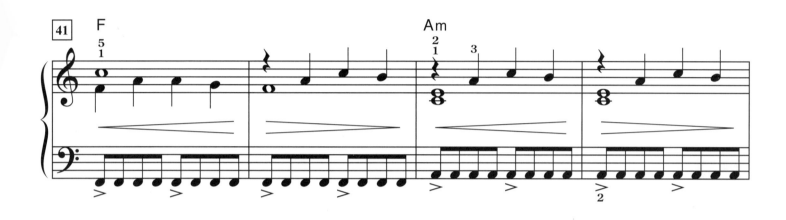

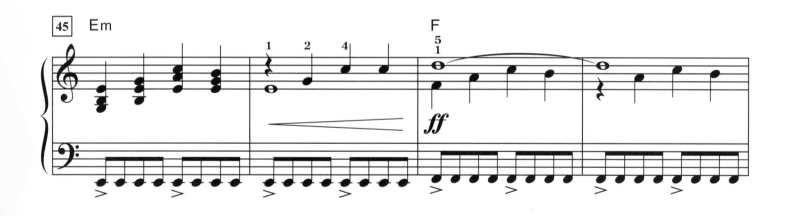

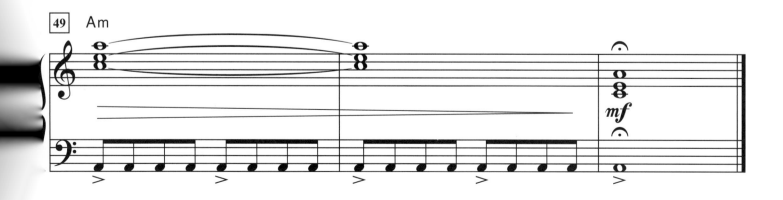

HEART BY HEART

(from *The Mortal Instruments: City of Bones*)

Words and Music by Diane Warren
Arr. Dan Coates

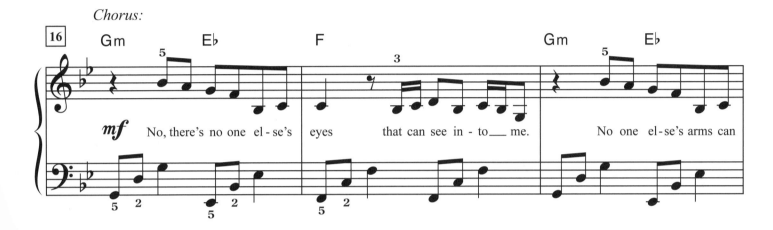

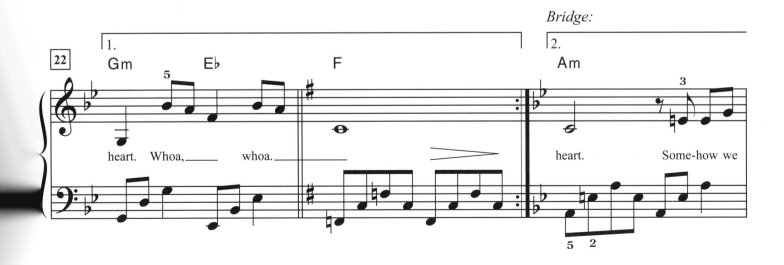

found a way to find each oth - er. Some-how I found my way to you.

Chorus:

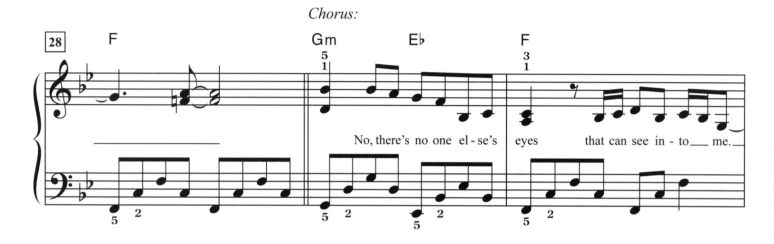

No, there's no one el - se's eyes that can see in - to___ me.

No, there's no one el - se's eyes that can see in - to___ me.

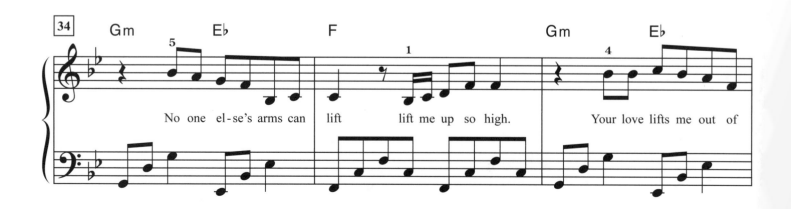

No one el - se's arms can lift lift me up so high. Your love lifts me out of

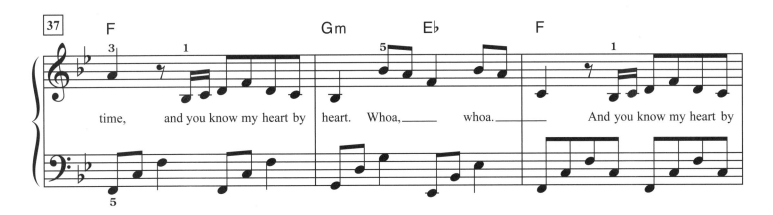

Verse 2:
When you're one with the one
You were meant to find,
Everything falls in place,
All the stars align.
When you're touched by the love
That has touched your soul,
Don't let go.
Someone comes into your life,
It's like they've been in your life forever.
(To Chorus:)

I SEE FIRE

(from *The Hobbit: The Desolation of Smaug*)

Words and Music by Ed Sheeran
Arr. Dan Coates

Verse 1:

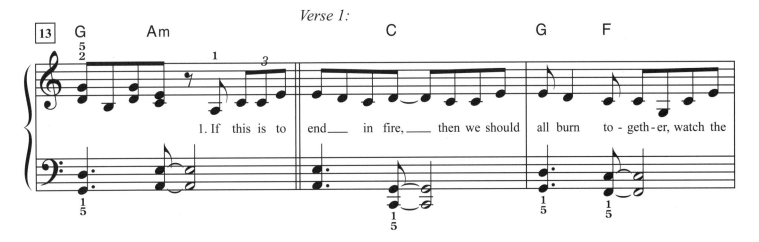

1. If this is to end____ in fire, ____ then we should all burn to - geth - er, watch the

flames ___ climb high_____ in - to the night.____ Call - ing out fath - er, _____ oh,

stand by and we____ will watch the flames burn au - burn on the moun - tain side.___

Verse 2:

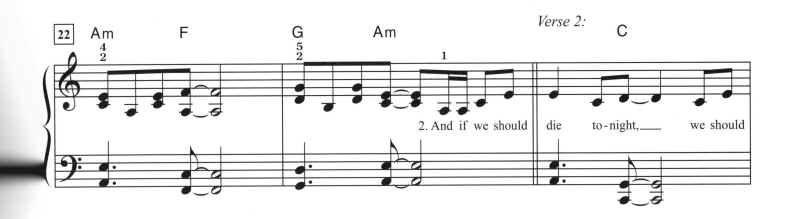

2. And if we should die to - night,___ we should

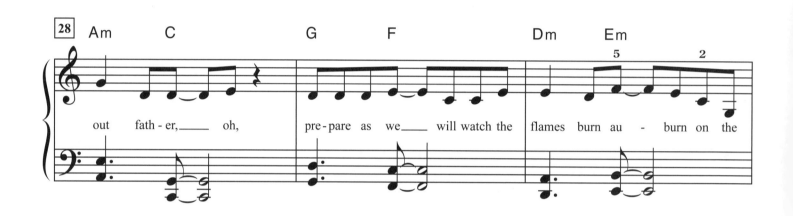

Chorus:

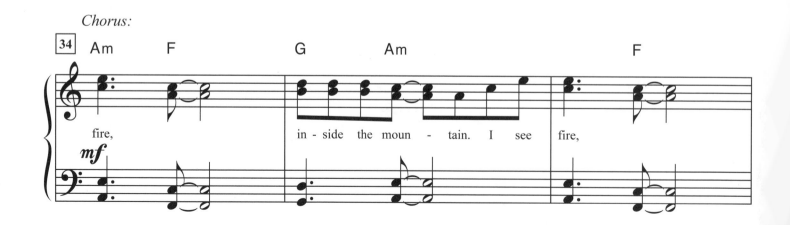

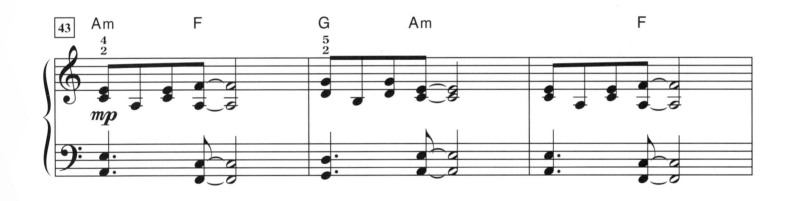

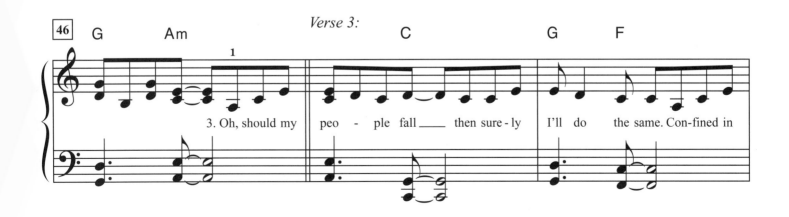

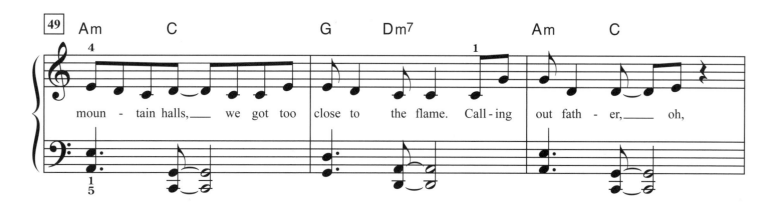

ROAR

Words and Music by Katy Perry, Bonnie McKee,
Max Martin, Lukasz Gottwald and Henry Walter
Arr. Dan Coates

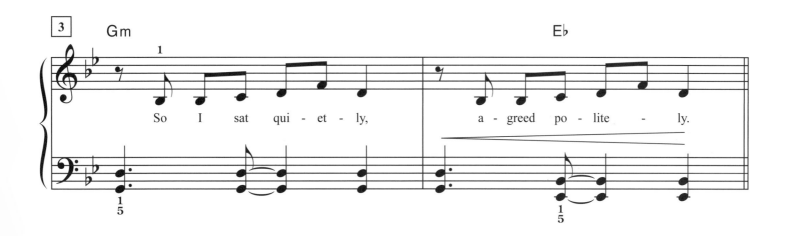

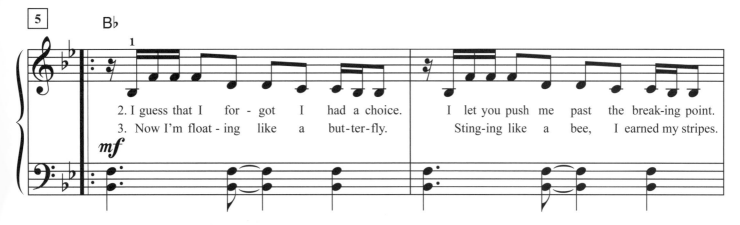

104

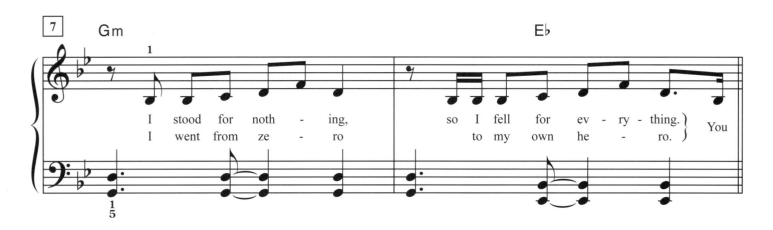

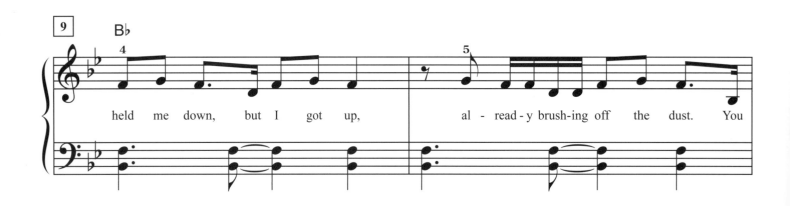

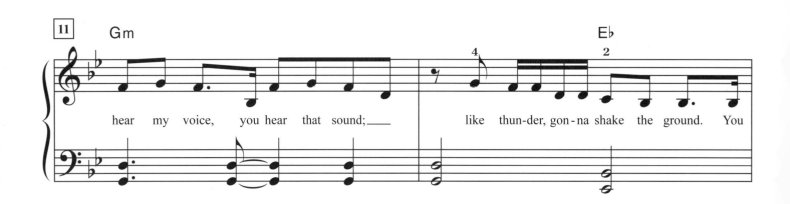

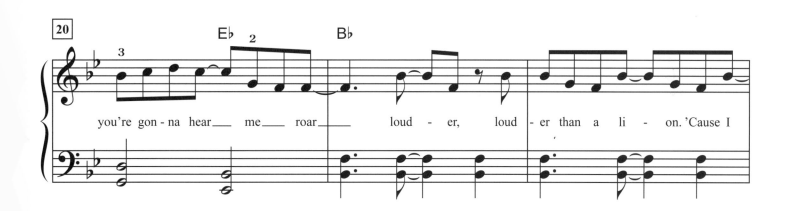

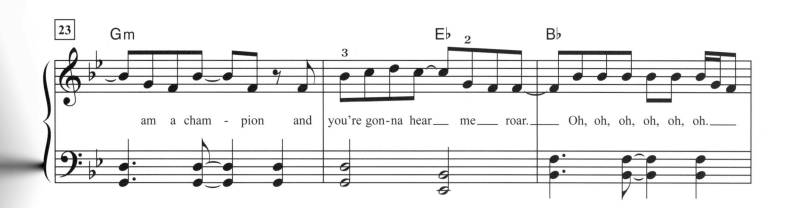

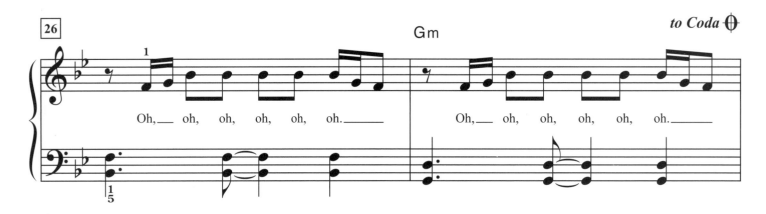

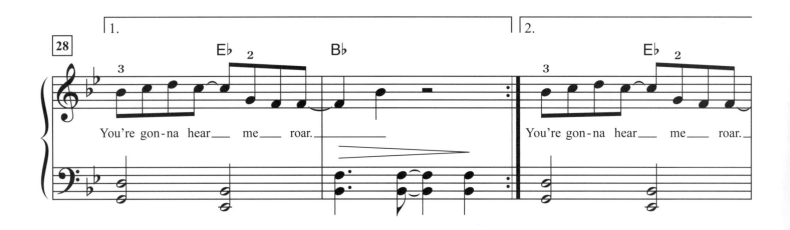

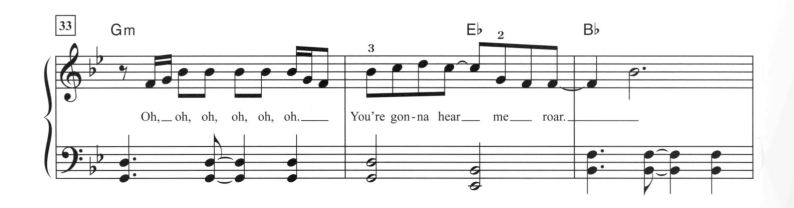

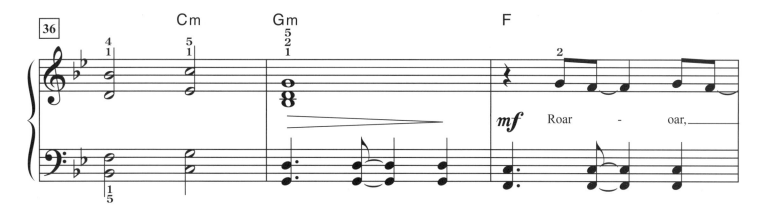

UNFINISHED SONGS

Words and Music by Diane Warren
Arr. Dan Coates

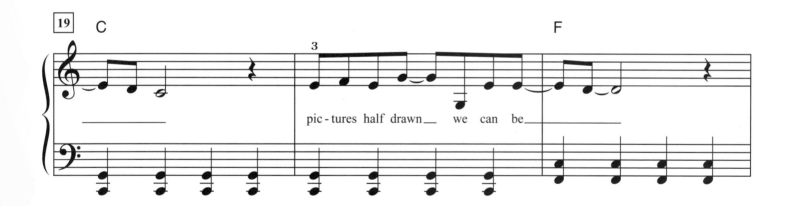

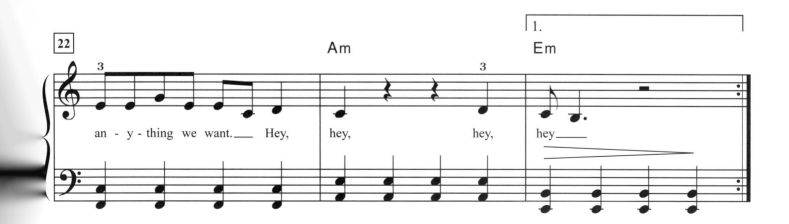

UP ALL NIGHT

Words and Music by Brett Beavers,
Jon Pardi and Bart Butler
Arr. Dan Coates

Moderate country rock

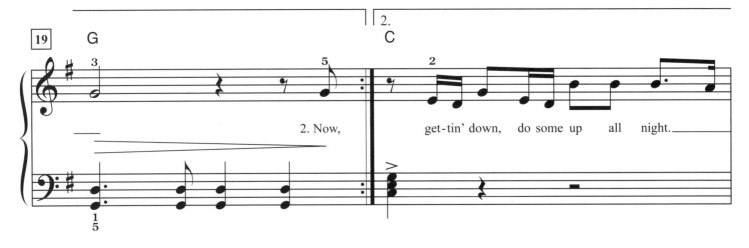

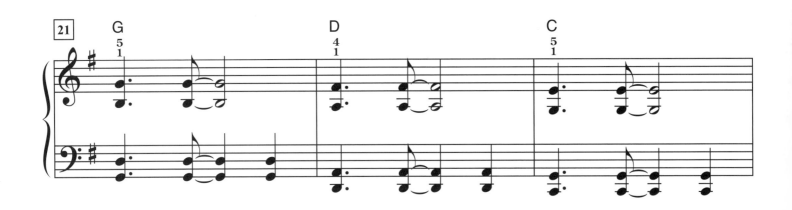

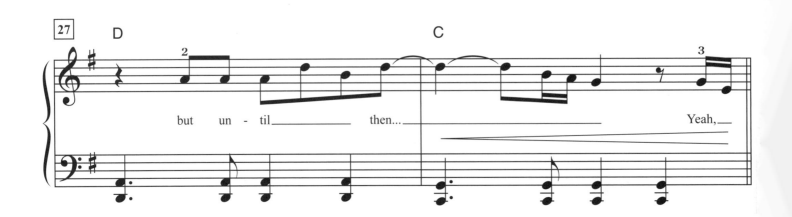

Verse 2:
Now, don't forget your flip-flops.
We can stop at a Quick Stop,
Get some jerky and a 12 pack.
No tellin' when we'll be back.
I gotta cooler in the bed,
Couple towels when we get wet
'Cause you know we're gonna jump in
And take a little midnight swim.
(To Chorus:)